Knickpoint

M.B.F. Wedge

Whisk(e)y Tit
NYC & VT

Copyright ©2018 by the author.
ISBN 978-0-9996215-6-1
Library of Congress Control Number: 2018933265

Cover painting by Jack Warren.

Knickpoint

A Memoir

Contents

"...the stories I want to tell you will light up part of my life, and leave the rest in darkness. You don't need to know everything. There is no everything. The stories themselves make the meaning.
The continuous narrative of existence is a lie. There is no continuous narrative, there are lit-up moments, and the rest is dark."

Jeanette Winterson, *Lighthousekeeping*

"Should I dream you afraid so that you are forced to save yourself?"

Joy Harjo, "She Remembers the Future"

Knickpoint

: An abrupt change in slope or gradient of a river, often characterized by waterfalls or rapids over hard rock areas. Caused by an uplift of land or a drop in sea level leading to rejuvenation.

I fell in love with my high school Earth Science teacher when I was fourteen and even my best friend laughed.

I stole the would-be geologist's lead sinker plumb bob
from his classroom and hung it in my locker:
early infatuation's vertical reference line.

When his coffee cup shattered by accident one study
hall morning
I thought about taking a shard from the garbage—
I'm attracted to men more familiar than most with the
crack-up of pieces
the subject of parts swept away.

Which of the details together amount to a cause?

How can anyone say where the story begins? Whisper, with the father, whose two little brothers died when he was a boy. No, say with the mother, who lost her footing and fell two stories to rocks when she was a girl. Say in the city where you, child, were born. Say none of these things. Start there.

All fall I write letters to Paul Calder Fisk who lives in an indigo house on Bridge Street, two blocks up from the river where, in September, the salmon run.

All fall Paul's instincts are slipstream: boulder bullet in a flume of brown.

Chemical Erosion: Oxidation: Rust. There's lead in the gun factory water where teenagers come of age.

9

I met Paul at a church event eleven days before I turned sixteen.

I shaved my teenage pubic hair for him in the bathtub the night before he visited my house the first time, three weeks in. He had asked me over the phone to do it, and an hour, thirty minutes before I made him come in my bed, my parents downstairs, he looked at me, smooth, and said, "I really feel like a pedophile now."

Something pulled open, gently, in the abiding dark.

Later, in the second floor storage room at his father's house, he'd press me, wet, against the wall next to the baby things no longer used.

who should be loved, and how. And how much.

We came to know each other better in the front porch days, my legs across his lap, passing our time easily on the couch in the shade.

Our paternal grandfathers were ball turret gunners in B-24 Liberators in World War II.

Thirty missions, fifty missions

when my grandfather flunked out of flight school, they assigned him to the bubble at the bottom of the plane.

Later I'd send Paul a CD with one song on it that
said

I think of you and think of flying.

Paul gives me a photograph from his childhood, sullied a little with circular scuffs, as if once caught under a spinning chair's foot, a studded snow tire turning in place on a concrete drive.

In fleece footie pajamas Paul holds a new pair of roller skates up, four chunky wheels and a red rubber crutch-foot brake on each. The boy I will love one day smiles brightly, even here, in spite of some poverty of spirit, yet unnamed, hovering just outside the frame.

When Paul was a boy and shattered his hand playing in the street, did he run and plunge it into the river to slow the swelling? Did he cry before his father consented, days later, to drive him to the hospital?

The first answer he gave me, when we met, about the scar: "I punched through my friend's football mask."

The rough and shiny webbing zipping up his hand.

A stone wall holds up the corner of Paul's yard. Does he still walk past it to sit by the water when the days get cold? Is he still afraid of being on the crumbling jumping bridge when it collapses, or does he find sanctuary there?

What happens to the permanent metal screws in your
bones when you grow?

It's the rock bottom beneath the barreling current, the fight of his life, that galvanizes Paul's phosphorescent heart and salmon skin.

I know something's wrong but not what. How do I admit to missing the signs?

Tweet, March, Paul:
"Getting harder and harder lately to do the right thing."

Vacation: half way around the world, twelve hours ahead that spring in the gazebo dining room where the stray gray cat now tame with the lightning bolt tail, broken, leaves a footprint on the red linen napkin at the top of the pile.

I will return after the tsunami wipes this breakfast bar into the sea.

Summer, Paul.

MDMA.   (3,4-methylenedioxy-methamphetamine) popularly known as Ecstasy, is a synthetic, psychoactive drug that has similarities to both the stimulant amphetamine and the hallucinogen mescaline. It produces feelings of increased energy, euphoria, emotional warmth and empathy toward others, and distortions in sensory and time perceptions.

The Popular Term, "Molly," (slang for molecular) refers to the pure crystalline powder form of MDMA, usually sold in capsules.

Summer, Paul.

His father calls; the connection is bad. His father takes him socks and shirts in jail and the seasons of my next number of years, his next number of nights in a place where even the convicts would cut him if they could are a telescope in reverse; the lines that have transmitted this news hang heavy over our heads and distort the graying distance of the sky on purpose.

I'd have written another man off in seconds for so much less.

He writes me one response. One initial missive on yellow-lined jail paper exposing what he's done and one letter more. Ever. Only.

An incongruous mix of curved capitals and lowercase littles: he swears he only looked.

The adult and the eight-year-old girl.

He and I both know how much worse it could have been.

Feeling: they will commit him I am committed I commit his crime for him by whispering his childhood nickname in his ear.

I never stop wanting him

I dream him on my body, heavy and warm like stones in a tranquil room.

Truth: I can't think about him when I masturbate: there are flashes of children

I dream him in my dress at the river

Pound's translation of "Exile's Letter" sewn into the seams.

He is released into his father's care.

In the middle of October, I cross the state before dawn in dangerous love, Paul flooding my system as the day's events unfold.

Mix tape, my grandmother's funeral. Hugs are OK touches, and shouldn't they be?

What part of me is still-always a child?

I have a hard time discerning what is appropriate; I know if you rub a dog too long in one spot it hurts.

Why does every part of this moment, except the dying, feel so wrong?

Venison on the counter above the peg and plank floors they've built themselves.

Paul labels the Ziploc bags. *Stake*, he writes, childish and defiant. "There's a deer in the village that everybody loves," he says, "she even has her own Facebook page: Bella Deer. Look it up."

Meet. Dear.

He smells to me like blood and roughed-up metal
like briny bones stripped
and left out overnight

cunt complement, contraction—

I have a lot of trouble reconciling reality with sense.

Last year my grandmother asked my father over Cheerios, "Do you know where this banana came from?" and he said "Yes. The store. I brought it over for you this morning." But she said "No. I happen to be the executive secretary of an international consortium of nations, and every month they send their dues. Sometimes they send money, and sometimes they send actual, physical goods. For instance, this month, Japan sent this banana."

We used to spend Thanksgiving with her when she lived alone but she drank too much scotch and required my parents to sleep in separate beds.

The last time I saw Paul we

Now I take him jars of soup made during the week after work; his home is along the way to the town where my grandmother used to live.

I want to trace his lightning lifeline, to warm the pins by friction I know are always cold.

To blast the hiding place of distance out of which another person might have made a shield.

Paul's father owns a decommissioned ambulance, painted blue. I'll hate myself later for asking Paul if he goes after children in the van.

I imagine the shell of him
back behind the razor wire in the yard
secrets coursing out and open now
slicing their way to his family
my god

One day
when we're safe
we'll speak frankly of force
but for now:

the stream table system has shifted
and I am afraid.

A Piece of the Sky

36

Mechanical erosion: The particulate breakdown of rock or soil into clastic sediment (geologic detritus) which is then transported elsewhere by the surface processes of water flow or wind.

At toxic levels, mood stabilizers scrub the human system in the blood.

Piss in the bathtub. Piss in the stoppered sink. There's piss in the parking garages in this city too but I would get paid five dollars an hour more to take care of it there. August and I work together for a while in a yellow house on a street that begins at the fire station, cleaning and sweeping and scrubbing away debris as if this were the catacombs and under the bones we'd find the entrance to hell itself. Certain stories are not to be repeated, understood? Certain warnings, certain five alarm bells, I ignore.

The extra set of keys for the yellow house hangs in our rehabilitative housing office downtown. There are somewhere near thirty sets of keys hanging here, each corresponding to an apartment leased in the city on temporary behalf of a person or persons who is, who are, said to be mentally ill.

Breakdown.
My mother and aunt work in mental health.
Let's call it lineage city.
It's how I get the job.

August is the housing manager and forgets his on-call bag in the back of my mother's car. They work for different agencies but ride together; he needs the phone in the briefcase for emergencies at night.

If no one answers, leave a message. If no one calls back in fifteen minutes, call again. Repeat if necessary. Call 9-1-1 if necessary.

He makes a special trip to get it back from her because someone always calls.

I go along with them in the car to my dusty job archiving paleontological volumes one day a week in the spring.

He insists on sitting behind me; he falls asleep slumped over the middle on warm afternoons.
"You're better than that job," he says, "and you know it, or you wouldn't be looking for something else."

I have a brother, but August, for a time, is like the son my mother never had.

Deposition: build-up of sediments, soil, and rocks resulting from loss of kinetic energy in water or wind.

After a form interview, August hires me to work for him at the rehabilitative housing office downtown.

Build-up:

Sometimes he buys me black gas station coffee in a paper cup.

I try to be disinterested in August. I scowl out the car
window mornings all summer long as a defense, but
a tension builds: a fondness I didn't intend.

The lion is most handsome when looking for food. Rumi

I have a husband, but this is not the point.

I wonder if Paul could be right for rehabilitative housing. "Can't be a sex offender," August says.

If you bite your fingernails enough, it's possible to damage your front teeth, I notice.

After hours, I fill the back of the rehabilitative housing office van with bricks from a demolition site nearby. There are birds in a book I read once who are called to the scene when something significant needs to be cleaned: scavengers, sort of, but in removing the unsightly or difficult material, these particular apparitions have the unfortunate tendency to rip rather too much away. Sometimes they take a piece of the sky by mistake.

I redistribute the bricks to the edge of our office's garden, but I am unable to restore what is missing above our heads.

48

My mother dreamt me out of Chernobyl. I was born exactly nine months after the Ukrainian nuclear reactor accident, three weeks early. Conceived, she says, after fifteen years of trying, just as the radiation cloud reached my parents where they lived.

Don't. don'tdon'tdon'tdon't*don't* say we're moving,
mom, I love my home.
Like that: Not cancer; say "more tests." Say "cure."
Two holiday hospitals, two surgeries in December.

Little soldier, I.
Deserter from the Navy.

August and I ride together without my mom, whose chemotherapy treatments now interfere with her work.

Caroline

Somewhere outside the city
after the freshly cooled air has shocked the leafy trees
I wonder if the circling snowflakes, barely formed
that miss the car like stars
will witness this moment
me laughing because you are here
the galaxy awaiting
like Oz

August plants images of kisses like seeds.

I have a husband, but this is not the point.

I say, "I don't think perfect love exists without perfect tragedy."

Kings of Leon, Isle of Wight, August says he knows me better than I know him.

We drive through Caroline a second time, morning after the first, morning after the rain that came later froze onto the trees and the storm had moved most of the way away. This is our crystalline Bavaria; the actual poem is never the one I had planned.

My husband and I hire the garbage department to roll a dumpster on our lawn: to catch the scraps launched out the windows of our disintegrating lives. Plural, *lives*, not singular. Wallboard in snow dissolves to paste; we handle the demolition ourselves.

Clover-leaf curve, close to the dwelling we thought we could love into something grand. The bridge barrier guardrail seems a simpler construction: the wrist-twitch, the wreckage; the outward and visible sign.

More than once in these hours, I overhear August say
"Stage four. And there is no stage five."

We become the cancer-patient-parent twins.

I try to send text messages, but they keep coming out in hand signals. I want you, but not like this. Blood transfusions and missed coffee dates at Christmas.

At New Year's, my mother's birthday, I want to sit in the rain by the river; I want to pretend I am drifting downstream.

Rehabilitation

One of the most difficult concepts to apply in river restoration or rehabilitation is the idea that each river is a uniquely functioning ecosystem, dynamic in space and time.

At work, the state Office of Mental Health requires all clients to prove, every year, that they are capable of preserving their own lives in an emergency.

I say:
"Name some ways you will tell if there is a fire in your apartment."
One resident responds, "See smoke."
"What else?"
"See flames."
"Ok. One more?"
Thirty seconds or sixty minutes or thirteen years pass with no response.

"What do you do if you are in the LIVING ROOM
and your HALLWAY is on fire?"
"Get a ladder, go down it."
"Where are you going to get the ladder?"
"Good point."
We have the same conversation, bullet for bullet, the
following day, and the following.

The Lithium he takes is saving his life instead.

Early on, I volunteer at a conference for adult survivors of childhood sexual abuse at the city's Holiday Inn.

August pops in at the beginning, disappears.

A hotel guest, or maybe a man off the street, wanders over to the table where I am selling the book for survivors, takes in the title, and says, "What a bunch of faggots."

A man with a nervous condition open sores on his legs and sometimes I share the couch with his scabs. Enough bright light exposure can lessen even the most serious scars.

We hire a cleaning service to get the blood off the walls. I learn to handle the psych unit checkouts on my own.

Master's degree, paella, I learn that saffron is more expensive by weight than gold.

Once in a while, these bright gems.

Maintenance man Sherman, who fiddles under sinks, folds his feet beneath his hulking frame on the floor like a child.

Schizophrenic mirror writing, cheekbone tattoo, fox fur left on the fire escape in the rain.

"Well, I just went over to free lunch at Loaves and Fishes; it was a madhouse."

"What, did they run out of salt?"

"No. They had too much of it and they were pouring it in everybody's wounds."

Bedroom TV splashed with semen, Aldi's bag filled with used condoms and hung on a nail by the bed.

Whoever fights monsters should see to it that in the process he does not become a monster. And when you look long into an abyss, the abyss also looks into you.
Nietzsche

Abstract thinking test:

"Shallow brooks babble. Still waters run deep."
"I can't imagine what that means."

We keep the controlled substances in a double-locked
cupboard.
Valium, Restoril, Suboxone.

I find a Xanax oval on the floor.
"Wanna split it?" August asks.

I'll split my mother's pills and take them, later, as she
dies.

I watch a young man die. As if it were possible to die more than once. As if the "once extinct" Washington Wolverine were capable of "making a comeback," as the weekend *Times* proclaimed.

August winks at me sadly over the body of the ventilated boy, and we talk to him. I describe last autumn's dresses from a magazine.

In spite of myself, I give up the certainty to which I cling.

What is this extinction, anyway?

Car dreams now, all the time. Standard transmission; I shift through the gears in my sleep. My two o'clock Tuesday writes everything down, underlines it, and boxes it in. Takes pictures of road signs and historical markers and the rules for the community swimming pool and prints the gritty home screen of her email page every time she opens it up. If she can catalogue it all, she'll understand it all; better to be crazy than stupid, she thinks. She tantrums. Drives her car faster than she should in the city; it's rumored she hit someone once in a crosswalk who happened to be in her way.

The maps of the city maintained by the records department downtown are supervised closely, copies given out only on special request. Once I was encouraged to look closely and think carefully about what the control of a landscape might mean, but all I can think of to do with this copy, today, is write "porch church," and "steel-deck," and "lover" on certain streets, as if naming the things that held weight would make them more possible for a person to own.

Gorge-bridge jumping suicide prevention meeting, city high school, seven PM.

Elected officials, concerned individuals, mental health care professionals, college advocacy groups, reporters, and a woman my mother knew once who says "what about guns?"

"Our greatest asset is our greatest liability," maybe they say, and I don't notice it now but later I will, the blending, the topographic transference of beauty and risk from landscape to being alive in this town.

I read August poetry in February and take liberties
with the responses he does not give. I get hung up on
the part of the movie *The Visitor* in which the white
woman asks the black woman where in Africa she is
from.

"Senegal."

"Oh!" the white woman says, too loudly. "I was in
Cape Town two winters ago!" as if discovering
they come from neighboring towns. "It was just
beautiful."

Taking liberties.

I get a text message from Paul early on the
fourteenth of February that says "happy VD,"
and what else can I do but laugh?

In the car that Valentine's morning with August I let
something I shouldn't slip.

Later he tells me he dreamt he was in my mouth, hard
enough to make me sick.

On my face, redness of heat and shame
from wanting.

Later I steal images of similar acts
implied.

Ships in the Night

"You're ten thousand miles away today," I say to August, one of the afternoons he's altered the route to make our trip longer, to spend more time, or to escape the weight of his daily routine, or to go by the house of a woman he used to love, or to avoid something, I'm never sure which. "Yeah," he says, "I am." And maybe I ask him what's wrong or maybe he says simply, "I'm worried." And I ask, "About what?" and he says, "My dad." And I notice the length of his arm, next to me in the sun and I want him to stop, to touch me, to pull over slowly and face me, to face the thing that makes him most afraid.

84

We are amidst the dying, but haven't accepted it yet. We sniff at the edges like dogs, but instead of rolling, for now, we run. In the Methodist church over the weekend my husband and I donate blood in return for the pints pumped into my mother all spring to make her strong.

The donation doesn't hurt, but by Monday half my arm is blue, then green: my own internal sea pulled to the surface by Saturday's super moon. Pouring out not only of my arm in some good deed, but rising in my murky chest.

Drowning in love is still drowning.

Surprise, and act of aggression, both; Monday morning, west, I make a move to escape the hastening dead that grasp at my heels.

Before even saying "Good morning," I kiss August carefully on the mouth in his dying father's car and when I move away he says *what* stop was *that* stop and I spend fifteen minutes trying to explain but neither one of us hears what I'm saying and then at the red light he says

"Kiss me again."
And I say, "I can't."
And he says, "You have to."

"No."
"Yes."
"No."

and I am no longer the person I was and later he says,
"I thought you were going to hit me."

Blister-pack heart: bubbles broken daily doling out a product I can't guarantee.

Derelict barn in the background; how many times over will I write this scene?

I had a pair of red shoes once.

A different man points out a woman in a different story who gets obsessed with the idea of pricing things: the groceries for the week, for instance, that makes sense, but the cost of the family cat, tallied, less so, especially after they've had him eleven years; she prices the value of her teenage son's date's tiara, secretly, after they've gone out the door and standing here I wonder about the value of two positively charged persons, facing each other for the first time, one foot apart, in the May afternoon:

I wonder about the cost.

We iterate, reiterate the awake-overnight shift in our coffee-stained clothes. I shoot my arrows over the homes of the dying; he conducts his business in the suit he wears to funerals.

My navy blue dress has a lion sewn into the tag. I choose it from the rack at the store and wear it for August who has put on his lion heart skin to honor the newly dead.

I listen to him speak about his father's life and wonder when he did this writing, at what point in the weeks of anticipating this moment he came close to the eloquence pouring over his audience now.

My mother asks me to read a Roethke poem when she dies instead of something I wrote.

After the service I hear August asking a friend to go to his home and find him some different clothes. He wants to get out of the suit. He wants to stop being the one demanded to set the tone.

I dream brush fires lick the edges of your house for days.

You're torn between wanting to save the world
And single-handedly burning it down.
How beautiful to watch the embers

He'll wear that suit or one like it on Halloween years
from now,
the family simulacrum:
they all dress dead.

How can a letter be written without any words? Why is a raven like a writing desk? A retraction, the ink. Shoved under his door in anemic defiance of the moment, days after the funeral, when from an overturned tire in my husband's garage I say into the phone, "I'm sick in love with you and I can't be." The single moment he says something back, cell phone reception spotty enough on the back roads he's driving he can ignore that he said it, categorically, forever. Two weeks.

Two weeks and in that time he'll say, "What's it going to take to get that look off your face?" and I will leave work early and he will tell me to take a few minutes and then come back because I still have two weeks worth of work to do.

I write that second-kiss scene in front of the falling
down barn, now swollen with summer heat.

I want
you to photograph me
in front of the bone-bleached and splintering boards
to keep your attention
until the sun makes my body a fever agreement
searing accessory
tender crime

The joining summer. I dream the woman who owns the property by the creek where you and I spend a couple of long afternoons is losing her memory. And what if she stops writing the animals and grasses and tiny events she sees happening here when she walks because she no longer remembers this place? She will forget us as she has forgotten her children: the water rippling against the current in the sunshine and wind; me dog-paddling, face up and shining, away from you in the cold on the hottest day. She will forget the turns I take back to you, a little downstream, the tips of our fingers, our lips that pass in the invented hours.

99

"Don't," he says.
 "What?"
  "Don't do that."
   "What?"
    "Don't laugh."

100

Wild, now, from clavicle to floating rib. The
morning following I dream a consummate oration,
delivered in my car and timed so perfectly the force
of spoken spinning resonates
centrifugal.

August and Paul share the date:
birthday, sobriety, one minute apart,
the peak of the Perseid Meteor Shower.

Wrap myself up in the darkness shot through with
stars
(this flaregarden nightshade can kill you)
to watch the incandescent rise
the dusk-struck dreams of evening
fall.

They punch at people in their sleep.

Beth

104

I promise this will be the first day in over a year that August and I don't speak. I'm trying to let sleeping dogs lie. *Start small*, I think, *just make it a day*. But brightly, when he calls, I offer him something sincere. "Are you with your mother?" he asks.

And I say "Yes," and "why?" and he says "May I speak to her?" and I say, "What's going on?"

And he says "Please give the phone to your mom," and I cross the street in front of the fountain in the center of town and extend my hand to my mother who is wearing a handkerchief on her head because the wig makes her scalp sweat, and itch.

Maybe he calls to silver the mirror, to break something, and maybe I let him because I want to be held.

Which of the details together amount to a cause?

My teacher brother once rescued a deer caught in the net of a goal on the field outside his classroom window.

A bus driver swerves to miss an animal in the road and crashes, extricating only himself from the freezing river where all the children are trapped. The smallest boy's unselfish heart gives out in the saving; raw story movie moments turn into days of tears.

Here is my mother, crossing herself

Here is my brother, detaching

there is no one to free us or gather us in.

There is nothing to do but wait. I exchange the heat of the wood-burning pizza oven restaurant for the cool of summer dusk; from the parking lot I speak to August on the phone a second time. "You're the only one I want to talk to," I say, and I can hear the heavy pleading in his voice when he replies, "you have to talk to your husband," and later, "but does it almost feel like you can't breathe?"

My mother and aunt work in mental health.
It's how August learns my aunt is sick before us when
we're out of town.

Her surgery is over now, she's resting, but I keep
thinking we could have been there sooner if we'd
known. Why has she insisted on a trickle-down
diffusion of this news?

When I was three I had a rubber ring pool floatie flamingo and I couldn't say the word right yet so it came out mamingo and I took it along on vacation to the rocky Rhode Island shore. I cried when the surf was too rough to play in and then after that when my lips got blue and my mother and aunt made my brother and me come out. I gave my mamingo water to drink from a bucket.

My aunt ended up with a lawn-ornament flamingo one Easter somehow and they never stopped showing up in her yard after that and everywhere else for that matter too, so she hated them good-naturedly, tried to give them away, wishing her friends would show up with penguins or loons instead.

She took us to Colonial Williamsburg for spring break when I was thirteen. A woman approached us in the Marriot parking lot from a van and trailer caravan and made some comment about how wonderful it must be to have a strapping young lad (my brother) to carry the bags. My aunt tried to be pleasant but she knew what was coming and when the woman asked

"Have you heard the Good News?"

my aunt looked her straight in the face and said "I've had just about enough good news for one day, thank you," and we loaded the bags in the back of the rented car and didn't come back.

When I bled through my underwear and khaki pants on the shuttle the second day because I didn't wear tampons yet and couldn't imagine that light colors might be a bad idea, a woman came up behind me and whispered in my ear and my aunt and my brother ferried me all the way back to the hotel in the heat and my brother said graciously nothing and my aunt asked if I felt alright, and then if I thought this was the first time something like this had happened in the history of world. Then if I thought it would be the last.

At the end of the day, the staff in each of the historical homes place the dining room chairs against the walls and roll up the rug. This they call "setting the room at ease."

The skin of her hands polishes silver.

Metastatic tumors: liver, lungs, and brain.

Runoff: movement of landwater to oceans by way of rivers, lakes, and streams.

Infusion tubes have drop factors.

Hospital cafeteria. Nerves on the surface like tree roots sticking out of a stream when the water is low: the stark exposure draws the eyes. The steroids make her talk for twelve hours straight for days—the history and benefits of eating chia seeds, for example; her little brother, David, who died fifty years ago after his car collided with a pony in the road. Her cousin Alan and I flank her hospital bed for a week in chairs.

Laughter a dry creek bed.

My aunt worries incessantly about finding a way to shave without nicking her legs. A bleed is an equal and opposite danger now to a clot like the one after the pony collision, the one that put her almost-100-percent-recovered brother in the ground.

August and I are cloistered, unavoidably, like two people stuck in an elevator with only so much air to breathe. Our separation doesn't separate us. He takes me up the hill to see my aunt before he goes to work. I steal sprigs of lavender from the hospital urns and press them in a book I've been meaning to give him, scaring myself by telling him I'd want him there if I were the one dying. I say I'd want to touch his face. And maybe I don't pick the lavender because someone has let it alone and maybe a night got too cold, just once; lavender tends to be an annual in this part of the world, unless you care very carefully for it. Even then, it doesn't always come back.

In front of spectators, Maggie Johnson piteously beseeches Pompous Pete. A sloppy rubbernecker recreates the scene, telling how she cried, "'did he love her, did he.'"

Secretly, I use all the words in all the arrangements I can think of, barring these.

He does not answer questions I refuse to ask.

I spend a week with my aunt at home following her surgery and I'm the only one allowed to touch her hair. Cousin Alan sends me out for groceries: zucchini, celery, carrots; fish and cream. He magics capers from her kitchen shelves, turns the fan on in my room and arranges a book of Basho on my pillow in the bed with the starflower sheets. He had a daughter my age who died in a freak accident when she was twenty and I was nineteen. A car came up on the Las Vegas sidewalk, crushed his vacationing girl.

An anonymous someone in the personals section of Craigslist writes, "the bone mends, but is never the same," and I respond, less than anonymously, "we are made of mended bones."

The radiation damages my aunt's hearing and sight; she loses the taste for most food. Her friends take her out for meals she doesn't eat; she's invited to celebrations; she comes to the housewarming party held at my house a year after my husband and I move in. She attends a high school musical and later expresses how happy she is to have gone. "Even though I couldn't hear what was happening," she says, "it didn't matter. I laughed when everyone laughed. I could tell how proud the kids were to be doing this and that made up for what I lacked."

My aunt clings to her job with my hit-or-miss mother as long as she can, answering phones from a recliner she's ordered an hour or two a couple of days a week. When she finally concedes, she gives my husband her judge-grandfather's heavy leather and metal bench chair. He carries it out of the office, stuffing bursting the seams.

How do I say I remember August there in his work shirt in front of the portrait mirror and occupying a seat that is no longer hers?

How do I say the agency hires him to fill her space sharing the office with my mom?

127

The grief animal inhabits the corner of the little city coffee shop where I have taken a part-time job. A man who makes conversation regularly at the bar says out of nowhere (no—clearly enough in response to something I must have just implied): "I will never participate," then goes back to stirring the sugar into his porcelain cup.

I ask August what color his house is and he tells me he actually doesn't know. I remember the floor because it hurts less than his blue eyes gone soft.

My captain, we are taking on water. The tip of a tissue in a bubble of blood. Slap my face for the words that come out in a borrowed tone.

SEA

130

These are hidden depths and resources, especially those with which you were born, those that you inherited. The Sea (water) represents the lunar and the female, and it is a link between your place of birth and the lands to which you may have to go on your spiritual passage. It also represents that which is maternal and, of course, travel itself.

What, or who, is left
I tell him I am going
Aye, someday, when.

the treated copper finishings where the water runs
down
the slate shingles restored
to the only house on the block
they've decided to save

132

Airport parking lot arrival where another man lost his car,

sat rotting while his father's new ghost whispered directions from behind.

Subterranean sublet
first day's temperature fight
heat mirage
regeneration of bones
up from ground

Sakya Monastery, Friday evening, Greenwood. Blue breath, open posture, straight. In the three weeks that no one can touch me but me, I wander around a garden store at 85th. I don't have a garden (I used to) and maybe this is the point: to cultivate life in my hands and press it back up under my ribs on my own.

An antique store. A junk shop. The treasure I make from two nautical prints I should pay to ship home, but then I might not have wanted these cold water sailboats in this panorama—here.

Sound is a beautiful word for a body.

Palliate, attenuate, unpack.

Collin Anderson will crash in February and I will remember his carpool to class with beautiful, pregnant Claire; I will remember the little dead children whose names we invoked in Herrick and Jonson and Donne; I will say out loud in the damp I am sorry for coveting what he had.

And no man is an island, oh this I know
But can't you see, oh?
Maybe you were the ocean, when I was just a stone

The flat map-distance is a deception; I will watch the colored diver training buoys drift in Alki shallows from the hill; his friends will light and stoke a vigil fire for him as he slips away.

I dream that we are deep-sea divers off a darkened shore.

My aunt is going to sail around the world. Always has been. In the last months of her life a stranger will deliver a map to her door with a box of bubble-top sewing pins. The souvenirs will arrive anonymously, too, filling her living room tables with tokens of light and weight, places immaculate, filthy, overwhelmed and deprived. She'll tack the pins to the countries, every week a new port in a foreign locale.

Zen Dog Tea House in Ballard; phone call for her birthday, two days after mine, two hundred fifty-four steps to Puget Sound. She will plan a late birthday party: incantations of water and pebble in gray. She'll be dead in two hundred fifty-eight days.

From the sidewalk in the sun:
Alexie's narrator will watch his cousin pistol-whip
and kill a man.

He will help him hide the body, gun.
Will climb on the roof of his house to sleep in the
cold,

wanting to be somewhere in response
he's never been.

A natural gas explosion at one forty-five A.M. will level the building, obliterate the coffee shop where I sit every morning drinking peppermint Northwest fog and Cardamom tea. The blast will blow the windows from the house around the corner where I sleep.

I'll write August a letter that says, "Do we scour the scrapyards?"

I take responsibility for accidents that haven't yet occurred.

They ask me to write the eulogy for Paul's funeral.
At least I imagine they would if he died.
As if it were possible to die more than once.
In a dorm room while my roommate slept, I taught
myself to orgasm.
I'm a little bit rough from the handling.

Ash Wednesday

Arterial Turns.
Some highway thing, or heart?
Put a cross on my head for holy homelessness.
Morning of impromptu friends departed
journey's anthem chanted, traveling.
Last look at city's skyline
traced with rain:
tragedy and love compel in other corners
just the same.

Change of Course

No net erosion occurs in late-stage rivers; the landscape is most often reduced to a flat, featureless surface that slopes toward the ocean.

In front of the bathroom mirror, back at my aunt's
house, I think

We shouldn't have asked her to stand here and brush
her teeth
(routine = sense)
We had to hold her, she whimpered
Why did we
You're not sleeping at all but damn you look good
today

Glowing I'd have said if I'd known

149

Three days of October sun
we speak softly
she waits for rain

I'm reading *Sons and Lovers* in the front room when it isn't my turn to sit up: the night they rearrange the furniture to accommodate a body laid out on the living room chairs.

She told me once she saw a casket-vision in front of these windows, exactly the place the couch I'll be sleeping on lies.

A gray neighborhood cat arrives at the front door in the fog

waits with me
I remember the back of the silent ambulance from the street
as if I had been outside

text message sent out at seven: "it's worse than that; she's dead."

Quiet, clean
how do we

set this room at ease

I take bells from her home in the morning and ring
them.

Now we become reconciled as you start away.

Alan slips fishing in North Carolina and breaks a
wrist.

Heart-shards, gestalt
He won't come to the funeral

But what of the mended bones?

Electric blue shirt, or is it a tie, to complement
August's eyes.
The funeral currency of a husband handshake, black
Jolly Roger bowtie
knowing what went on

I develop a single hive.

Storytelling in front of an easel at the luncheon I didn't arrange

"She told her brother they should have a portrait taken of the two of them to give their parents for Christmas. She made him wear a jacket, dragged him downtown to have it done. When their mother opened the framed print, this one, Christmas morning and started to cry, her brother, maybe it was only a few months before he died, said, 'I told you she'd hate it. What a stupid idea. We never should have paid all that money. This was the worst idea ever...' and she just sat there and beamed."

Your father's dead and so's my aunt:

Maybe they first noticed the change in their houses
Lungs the water whistles blown
when their warm body barometers
window-wire thermometers
started to rise

Phrases slip out; innuendos and unfulfilled promises
catch in the throat:

white t-shirt dreams cake like mud in our open
mouths.

The truth for a long while is I'll go back to that spot
to kiss him
back beneath starlings like water in the trees.

Thoracic spine, sternum.
Murmuration patterns, pain.

Rejuvenation

162

Evolution of landforms: when earlier surface features are
locally preserved, rejuvenated terrains are complex.

Ordinary occasions filter back into the jar
stacked with gravel events
like sand

Certain forms remain, as surely as some wear away.

Paul calls.

Living water sluices blue
like map lines, like veins;

for an hour he answers my questions, candidly, the
best he can.
Tuesday is sex-offender support group night.

I say I've never had more hope for him than I do now.

You suspect the floor we find under the carpet after
my mother dies is tight-grain, old growth yellow
pine.

Heartwood, it's called.

I get more than a little caught up with the worth of
reclaimed things
the day we almost can't bear not kissing.

Beyond the stairs like that, before, the broken spindles, lived raccoons.

Now instead the ravages, a leaking roof repaired above a light-filled if unfinished room.

Two nylon painters' caps hang in the window, street-side, the morning I visit alone; I wonder if he and she wore them and danced, silly and splattered, hoping the neighbors would look in and see they were hard-pressed but better for being in love.

It's fair to say I can't get past the house, but not only.

I drop the insulated foam board door ahead of us back
down the steps: grab after it, laughing, retrieve.

Have I been close enough to stroke his temples?
If/then, what then, when?

He describes us in words I shy away from, like
"addict," like "enabler," although he's right; they're
always true.

Before I leave I lie next to him in his downstairs bed
and think of the parting: lips and legs

of passages and flow.

The truth is I'll never stop loving you, roller skate
boy, despite what it does to me

for dying I'm sure now is only a subway train in a
city, approaching, from one stop away
the increase
until I am track static
and you, the tunnel of darkness

the channel of wind and sound.

I have come to a still, but not a deep center,
A point outside the glittering current;
My eyes stare at the bottom of a river,
At the irregular stones, iridescent sandgrains,
My mind moves in more than one place
In a country half-land, half-water.

After dark, Shef will take us swimming at the quarry
in the rain

Kristen, with her vodka on the log at water's edge
will learn that lightning struck her home while we
were gone
the trees will glow in the half-vision of a day-old full
moon
intermittently obstructed by clouds

I will howl, keening
electricity on line

171

Newer mythologies
inherit
that birthright bruise
the sky

172

Notes

Page 3 *"An abrupt change."* "River/Fluvial Revision Notes." The Geography Site, 22 Feb. 2006. www.geography‑site.co.uk. Accessed 30 Oct. 2016.

Page 12 *"who should be loved."* Roy, Arundhati. *The God of Small Things.* New York: HarperCollins Publishers, Inc., 1997. Print.

Page 13 *"I think of you."* Vatter, Jason. "Flying." *These Friends of Mine.* Lokel Yokel Records, 2000.

Page 22 *"MDMA."* "Drug Facts: MDMA (Ecstasy/ Molly)." National Institute on Drug Abuse, revised, February 2016. www.drugabuse.gov/drugs-abuse/ mdma-ecstasymolly. Accessed 20 Feb 2016.

Page 37 *"Mechanical Erosion."* "Erosion." BBC, 2016. www.bbc.co.uk/science/earth/ surface_and_interior/erosion. Accessed 30 Oct. 2016.

Page 43 *"Deposition."* Marshak, Stephen. *Essentials of Geology (4th Edition).* New York: W. W. Norton & Company, Inc., 2013.

Page 48 "Sometimes they take." Gaiman, Neil. *The Ocean at the End of the Lane.* New York: HarperCollins, 2013. Print.

Page 62 *"One of the most difficult."* Wohl, Ellen. *Disconnected Rivers: Linking Rivers to Landscapes.* New Haven: Yale University Press, 2004. Print.

Page 65 "book for survivors." Lew, Mike. *Victims No Longer.* New York: HarperCollins Publishers Inc., 2004. Print.

Page 73 "Whoever fights monsters." Nietzsche, Friedrich. Beyond Good and Evil: Prelude to a Philosophy of the Future. 4.146. Translated by Walter Kaufmann, Random House, Inc., 1989. Print.

Page 119 "Runoff." "Runoff: Transfer of landwater to the oceans." Department of Atmospheric Sciences at the University of Illinois at Urbana Champaign. ww2010.atmos.uiuc.edu/(Gh)/wwhlpr/runoff.rxml. Accessed 30 Oct 2016.

Page 123 "In front of spectators." Crane, Stephen. *Maggie: A Girl of the Streets. Great Short Works of Stephen Crane.* New York: HarperCollins Publishers Inc., 2004. Print.

Page 131 *"These are hidden."* Murray, Liz and Colin. *The Celtic Tree Oracle: a System of Divination.* New York: St. Martin's Press, 2015. Print.

Page 137 "And no man is." Howard, Ben. "Black Flies." Every Kingdom, Island Records, 2011.

Page 148 "No net erosion." "Evolution of Fluvial Landforms." Par. 5. *Indiana University.* www.indiana.edu/~g105lab/images/ gaia_chapter_12/fluvial_landforms.htm. Accessed 30 Oct. 2016.

Page 151 Lawrence, D. H. *Sons and Lovers.* Devon, England: Dover Publications, 2002. Print.

Page 163 *"Evolution of Landforms."* Dallmeyer, R.D. *Physical Geology, Laboratory Text and Manual.* Dubuque, Iowa: Kendall/Hunt Publishing Company, Inc., 2000. Print.

Page 170 *"I have come."* Roethke, Theodore. *"The Far Field"* (North American Sequence) The Far Field. Garden City, New York: Doubleday, 1964. Print.

Acknowledgments

I would like to thank my husband, Matthew Fiorelli, and our daughter, Rosie, for their ongoing love and support.

I'd like to thank Miette Gillette of Whisk(e)y Tit, for her immediate belief in and delicate, thoughtful handling of this book.

I would also like to thank Rebecca Utter, Jill Twohig, Cara Hoffman, Elena Georgiou, Richard Panek, Douglas A. Martin, and Michael Klein, without whom my life would be far less bright.

181

A note about the type

This book was set in Cardo, a font specifically designed for the needs of classicists, Biblical scholars, medievalists, and linguists. This font is the author's version of a typeface cut for the Renaissance printer Aldus Manutius and first used to print Pietro Bembo's book De Aetna.

About the author

M.B.F. Wedge holds an M.A. from the State University of New York at Cortland and an M.F.A. from Goddard College in Plainfield, VT. As well as a rehabilitation coordinator for the mentally ill, she has worked as a local foods delivery driver, a barista, and a house paint mixer. She lives with her family in Upstate New York. *Knickpoint* was a finalist for the 2017 Tarpaulin Sky Book Prize.

About the publisher

Whisk(e)y Tit is committed to restoring degradation and degeneracy to the literary arts. We work with authors who are unwilling to sacrifice intellectual rigor, unrelenting playfulness, and visual beauty in our literary pursuits, often leading to texts that would otherwise be abandoned in today's largely homogenized literary landscape. In a world governed by idiocy, our commitment to these principles is an act of civil service and civil disobedience alike.

9 780999 621561